IRIS
CUB SCC
HANDBOOK

TONY DAWSON

BLACKWATER PRESS

© Copyright text: Tony Dawson

First Published in 1996 by Blackwater Press,
Unit 7/8 Broomhill Business Park, Tallaght, Dublin 24,
Ireland.

Printed at the Press of the Publishers.

Editor: *Zoë O'Connor*
Design: *Philip Ryan*
Illustrations: *Marie–Louise Fitzpatrick, Philip Ryan*

ISBN 0 86121 822 1
British Library Cataloguing-in-Publication Data.
A catalogue record for this book is available from the
British Library. Dawson, Tony. Irish Cub Scout's Handbook.

THIS HANDBOOK BELONGS TO:

Name: _Lorna Slattery_

Address: ....

....

....

....

Date of Birth: ....

I joined cubs on: ....

I was invested on: ....

Badges I have earned

Badge	Date	Badge	Date
Artist		Athlete	
Bookreader		Collector	
Communicator		Cyclist	
Entertainer		Explorer	
First Aider		Fisherman	
Gardener		Handyman	
Hobbies		Home Help	
Map Reader		Musician	
Naturalist		Pathfinder	
Photographer		Rescuer	
Scientist		Sports	
Swimmer		World Conservation	

I was awarded the following arrows:

Bronze (date)_____   Silver (date)_____   Gold (date)_____

CONTENTS

·····················

WHAT IS A CUB SCOUT?

Welcome to this handbook of fun and games! As we hike through the pages, we'll meet cubs in their dens, running through woods, singing at campfires and many other exciting places. We'll join them as they take part in the fun and games which make cubs one of the most fun-filled ways of learning for boys and girls.

There are stories to entertain, jokes to make you smile, quizzes which will set you thinking, games to have fun with and a host of pages filled with ideas and information. Join with us as we make lanterns, use the morse code, learn about knots, cycle safely and take part in many other activities enjoyed by young people across the globe.

Cub scouts want to learn as much as possible about their world. Being helpful to people, young and old, makes a cub happy. The cub scouts know that their training, games, hikes and other activities will help them keep alert and healthy.

In these pages you will find how much cub scouting can do for you. More importantly, you will discover what you can do for cub scouting. As you will see, cub scouts learn to help each other in many ways. A great number go on to join scouts, and then become cub/scout leaders, and leaders in many walks of life.

Enjoy this book. If you are not already a member of the greatest youth organisation in the world – with currently over fourteen

5

million members – perhaps you will want to join after discovering the wonder and fun of cub scouting!

CUB BADGES AND ARROWS

During their years in cubs, boys and girls are encouraged to learn while having fun. While every activity they take part in ensures that they learn a little about lots of things, there are certain subjects they may become quite good at.

Tests are carried out in about thirty different hobbies. When cubs show they know something about these hobbies a special badge is awarded. These badges are worn with pride on their left sleeve.

Most of these badges are triangular in shape. Round badges are earned while working as a team. Triangular badges include First Aider, Book Reader, Scientist and Pathfinder. Round teamwork badges may be achieved for Entertaining, Camping, Conservation and other subjects.

Scientist

World Conservation

Other badges which may be earned are shown throughout this book, with information about their subject. Some badges, e.g. Athlete and Swimmer, are awarded in three stages. A different-coloured badge (yellow, green or red) is awarded for each grade.

Athlete

As a cub progresses she/he begins the Arrow Trail. This is a set work programme carried out during the cub years. Cubs are awarded a Bronze, Silver and Gold Arrow after passing a selection of about nine tests for each Arrow. The Arrows are earned about a year apart from each other. After gaining the Gold Arrow, cubs work for their Link Badge which brings them to the scouts. Arrows are worn around the Tenderfoot badge as shown.

Tenderfoot with Arrows

KNOTS

A good rope is a climber's greatest treasure. Every time they take to the hills these people trust their lives to the twisted fibres from which modern ropes are made. The correct knot must be used each time, otherwise the fibres will become worn and damaged sooner than expected. This will weaken the rope, possibly inside where the damage cannot be seen. The danger to a climber who trusts his or her life to such a rope is obvious.

Cub scouts are encouraged to take an interest in knot-tying. Some day they may join the venture scouts and be glad of their basic knot-tying skills. Here we look at some simple knots and their uses in everyday life.

The Reef Knot

Used to tie two similar ropes together or for tying parcels, this knot is usually the first that cubs learn. It is a very neat knot and will lie flat when finished, so it's ideal for tying bandages during first aid treatment.

The Reef Knot

Holding the rope ends in each hand, put the left end (a) over the right. Then pass the end (a) under the other end as you would when tying your laces, holding (a) under (b). Next loop end (b) over and under the other rope and pull both ends tight. You will notice that both ends of each rope lie on the same side of each loop.

Figure of Eight Knot
Used as a "stopper knot", this tie has many uses. It may be used to stop eyes slipping off a rope or to stop a rope from slipping through a hole or ring. As it is reliable with catgut or nylon, it's useful for violinists or people who fish.

The Figure of Eight Knot

Hold the rope end in your right hand. Pass it under and over the main rope (i). Then thread the rope end through the top of the circle (ii). Pull both ends to secure and finish (iii). Pulling on the rope ends will strengthen the knot, making it an ideal "stopper".

Highwayman's Hitch
A hitch is a way of tying a rope to an object without a full knot. The Highwayman's is the simplest of hitches and was used by highwaymen and cowboys.

It is used to secure horses or pets to a fence or pole.

Make a loop behind the fence, leaving about ten inches of rope at the free end. From the other side of the rope make another loop (ii) and pass it in front of the fence. Then push it through the first loop. Tighten this loop. Now take the free ten inches and make it into another loop. Pass this loop in front of the fence and through the second loop (iii). Tug the animal end of the rope to tighten the second loop.

The Highwayman's Hitch

Now your animal can tug as hard as it likes without undoing the hitch. However, a sharp tug on the free end of your rope will open it without any bother.

The Sheepshank
This is a knot used to safely shorten a rope or to strengthen a worn section in the rope. As in diagram (i), bend the rope twice as you make the letter "Z" with it. These bends are called "bights".

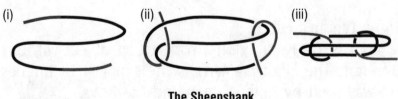

The Sheepshank

Diagram (ii) shows how to loop the free ends. Place these loops over the bight and tighten by pulling the free ends of your rope (iii). The tighter you pull the rope, the more secure your sheepshank knot becomes.

QUIZ – FIRST TWENTY

1 What is the scout sign for "Gone Home"?
2 What word begins with "P" and means very clean?
3 You are facing east when ordered to "Left turn, about face, right turn." Which direction should you now be facing?
4 It is a layer of gas protecting the earth from the sun, but it's being damaged by smoky fuels, petrol fumes and other man-made gases. What is it called?
5 Who lived at 221B Baker Street?
6 What bird lays its eggs in other birds' nests?
7 What is the difference between a burn and a scald?
8 What is the longest river in Ireland?
9 Name three Irish Youth Hostels in the surrounding district.
10 What picture is on the Entertainer's badge?
11 Name the world's highest mountain.
12 Make a Reef Knot. (Provide two pieces of rope for each team.)
13 In what month is Founder's Day?
14 Name one of your local shops, e.g. Butchers, Newsagents, Video Store, Hairdressers, etc.

15 What fruit could you use to make invisible ink?
16 What do you use to send messages in semaphore code?
17 Name three trees with three letters.
18 Who founded the scouts?
19 Name his friend who wrote *Jungle Book*.
20 What is a flying fox?

THE IMPORTANCE OF INSPECTION

When people think of cubs, they imagine groups of girls and boys running through forests and fields, muddy and sweaty, covered in grass and leaves as they romp through the trees. This is indeed part of what cubs are about. However, before the fun begins cubs are expected to be clean, neat and tidy. This is checked by your leaders during cub inspection at the beginning of each meeting.

Each cub is inspected for clean hands, face, neck, etc. Uniforms should be clean and neat. Neckerchiefs should be ironed, if possible, and free of creases and ratty ends. All badges should be sown into position – cubs are encouraged to sew on their own badges.

Of course, being healthy, happy people, cubs are expected to smile during inspection. It's wonderful to see so many sets of gleaming white teeth. Are your teeth clean and healthy now?

Two or three days before your club meeting check your uniform. See that it is clean and neat. If not, wash it yourself. Your parents, big brother or big sister will not lose points for their six if the uniform isn't up to scratch.

Have a shower or a bath before your cub meeting and make sure that your hair is combed – tie back/up any long or unruly hair.

Of course, when the meeting, hike, camp or other activity is over cubs are not expected to be so spotless. Remember, your cub meeting is not finished until you have cleaned yourself up at home!

RUCKSACKS AND THEIR CONTENTS

Before going on a hike or camp, all cubs will be advised by their leaders as to what to bring with them. This does not deter some newcomers from trying to stuff their favourite chair and the family television into their rucksacks. Usually, when this fails, it's because "the rucksack is too small"! A cub scout needs only to bring minimum equipment when hiking, camping or hostelling.

A good sleeping bag. A foam mattress is ideal for under your sleeping bag when hostelling.

A torch can give a great sense of security to newcomwers in dark and strange surroundings.

Warm pyjamas.

A change of clothes, including footwear, with a double change of underwear, if possible.

13

Cutlery. Knife, fork, spoon, plastic mug (metal mugs can cause nasty burns when filled with hot liquid).
Toiletries: Face cloth, towel, soap, toothbrush and toothpaste and a comb.
A small quiet indoor game, eg, draughts, ludo, chess, etc. Cubs should **never** carry penknives – they are too dangerous.

A strong but light rucksack should be used. The above equipment is meant to make your load as light as possible. Putting it all in a big heavy mountaineer's rucksack will only defeat the purpose.

Sleeping bags are contained in small sacks called "stuff sacks". It's a good idea to practise stuffing your bag into this sack in the comfort of your own home. All too often cub leaders spend the last half hour of camp stuffing their cub's sleeping bags into sacks before heading off, when the cubs should be doing this themselves!

FAVOURITE SONGS AND CHANTS OF CUBS

When walking through forests or sitting at a campfire, it's natural to want to share your cheerful mood with everybody within earshot. Here are a few of the many songs and rhymes often heard within shouting distance of a cub pack.

My Bonnie Lies Over The Ocean

My bonnie lies over the ocean
My bonnie lies over the sea
My bonnie lies over the ocean
Oh bring back my bonnie to me.
Bring back, oh bring back
Bring back my bonnie to me
Bring back, oh bring back
Bring back my bonnie to me.

This song begins with everybody standing in a circle. Every time a word beginning with "B" is sung all must bend knees and squat until the next "B" word is sung. Then all must stand up again. The song begins quite slowly but picks up speed as you go along. Try it and see who are the fittest people in your cub pack!

Head and Shoulders

Head and shoulders, knees and toes, knees and toes
Head and shoulders, knees and toes, knees and toes
And eyes and ears and mouth and nose
Head and shoulders, knees and toes.

Each time you say a body part you touch it with your right index finger.
   Repeat the verse, leaving out "Head" and sing faster and louder.
   For each verse sung, cut out a body part until you can only sing twelve "And"s.

15

Finally, sing the song again as quickly as possible.

Everywhere We Go-Oh

Everywhere we go-oh
(Repeat)
People always ask us
(Repeat)
Who we are
(Repeat)
And where do we come from
(Repeat)
And we always tell them
(Repeat)
We're from ABC town, XXth ABC town
And if they can't hear us
(Repeat)
We sing a little louder
(Repeat)

"ABC town" indicates the name of your town or village. "XXth" indicates the number of your scout troop.

Repeat whole song LOUDER! Repeat six or seven times, each time increasing the volume.

Finally, make the last line,

And if they can't hear us THEY MUST BE DEAF!

Indian Canoe Song

Hi, ho anybody home?
Food nor drink nor money have I none
But I will still be ha-ha-pip-pip-happy.

Begin the first line very quietly, when the Indian is way up river. Gradually sing louder as the canoe comes closer. Repeat the song four or five times until the Indian passes by. Then you reduce the volume, repeating it more quietly each time. As the Indian goes out of earshot reduce voices to a whisper. Finally, just mouth the words in silence.

Quartermaster's Store

There was milk, milk
White and clean as silk
In the store, in the store.
There was milk, milk
White and clean as silk
In the quartermaster's store.

My eyes are dim, I cannot see
I have not brought my specs with me
I have not brought MY SPECS with me,

There were cubs, cubs
Washing at the tubs
In the store, in the store.

17

There were cubs, cubs
Washing at the tubs
In the quartermaster's store.

My eyes are dim, I cannot see
I have not brought my specs with me
I have not brought MY SPECS with me

There was Rory, Rory
Telling a great story
In the store, in the store...*

*Continue as in verses above. Make up new verses with your friends' names and rhymes to accompany them.

Taps

At the end of campfire, all sing to the air of The Last Post as played at army camps at sunset and other times. Stand to attention with hats off!

Day is done
Gone the sun
From the sea
From the hills
From the sky
All is well
Safely rest
God is nigh.

CAMPFIRE FUN!

The campfire is also a time for cubs to entertain each another. Indeed, it presents a golden opportunity to earn your Entertainer badge. Here are some ideas for you:

Magic Trick – The Disappearing Hanky

The audience see you with a paper bag in one hand and a handkerchief in the other. You place the hanky in the bag, blow up the bag, then burst it and tear the bag in pieces. But where did the hanky go?

Setting Up: You need two paper bags large enough to hold a handkerchief. Using paste, stick the bags together side by side. Cut a "dip" out of the centre wall between the two bags. It now looks as though you are holding only one paper bag.

Place a hankerchief in bag "A". Blow into bag "B" and then burst it. Bag "A" will remain intact. Carefully tear the burst section of the bag while hiding bag "A" in your fist. Put the torn bag in your pocket, along with the hanky in the other bag.

The Disappearing Hanky

As with all magic tricks, this should be practised often before performing it in front of a real audience.

Chinese Whispers

This favourite among cubs shows the importance of clear speech and proper listening when in conversation. It is usual to tell the story of the army general before radio or telephone were invented.

Long ago a big battle was about to take place. The general in charge of one side needed more men. As they were some sixty miles from headquarters he sent a messenger on foot with the message, "Send reinforcements, we are going to advance!"

As messengers had to run through rough countryside, passing small outposts, they stopped at these shelters and repeated the message to another soldier who then brought it to the next fort.

The general's message was passed along by about ten or twelve people. Unfortunately the soldiers were so excited that each person changed it accidentally. Imagine the face of the general at headquarters when he was told a message had come from the battle saying, "Send thirty-four pence, we are going to a dance."

In this game all cubs sit in one big circle. The cub leader then whispers a short sentence into a cub's ear, for example, "The butcher fried onions with his chips." By the time this has passed through about twenty whispering cubs — who must only say the message once — it could become, "Bill's mother tried growing turnips."

Try it yourself and see what happens. You could be surprised – and amused – by the result.

Campfires are usually fun-filled and entertaining – without a television or stereo system to be seen or heard. Cubs and their leaders use their imagination as we have seen, to keep each other happy. Indeed there is no limit to the variety seen at campfires. Charades, animal noises, acting out a short play or sketch, are just some of the possibilities for a great night's amusement supplied by yourselves.

THE COMPASS

When hiking or camping it is important to bring a map of your area and a compass with you. Knowing how to use these will prevent you getting lost and can also show you the quickest way to your destination.

The needle of a compass is a magnet. This magnet is attracted by a strong magnetic force near the North Pole, so the needle always points north. A map is like a picture of an area drawn by somebody flying over it. A map will have an arrow drawn on it pointing north.

Placing your map on the ground with the compass over it will let you find the direction of your destination, provided you know where you are on the map and your destination is marked. Turn your map so that the north-pointing arrow is in line with your compass needle. If your target place

21

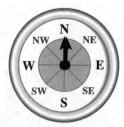

The Compass

is to the right of your present position on the map, you walk in that direction.

You should look for other clues on your map, like streams, hills, or forests, and keep an eye out for them as you go. That way, you'll know that you're heading in the right direction.

The main points of a compass are north, south, east and west. As you can see from our picture, other points are also marked. These are north-east, south-east, south-west and north-west.

Like everything else in cubs, there will always be an adult ready to help you. Ask your cub leaders; they are always glad to show how maps and compasses work.

FINDING YOUR WAY WITHOUT A COMPASS

It is possible to find the direction of north without a compass. During the day we use the position of the sun. At night we use the stars.

Using the Sun and Your Watch
Simply point the hour hand of your watch towards the

sun. Midway between the hour hand and twelve on your watch will point south.

For example, suppose it was half past four. The hour hand would be halfway between four and five. (Call this four and a half or 4.30.) Then midway between this point and twelve would be two and a quarter, or 2.15. This means that a quarter of the way between two and three points south.

For another example, suppose it was eight o'clock. With the hour hand pointing to eight, midway to twelve is ten. The direction that ten points to is south.

Due to the clocks being put forward in places using B.S.T., south is halfway between one and the hour hand when it points to the sun. (Summer time only.)

These instructions are correct for the northern hemisphere only. If you happened to be south of the Equator you would use different rules.

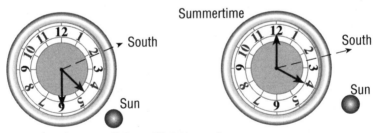

Using a Watch as a Compass

Using The Stars
On a clear night you can find your way by using the Pole Star. This star is always almost directly over the North Pole. It is also called the North Star.

Looking skyward you should see a set of seven stars forming the Plough. This is also called the Big Dipper. Close to this you should see a group of five stars, known as the Little Dipper. The two stars at the base of the Big Dipper are called pointers. These point towards the Pole Star.

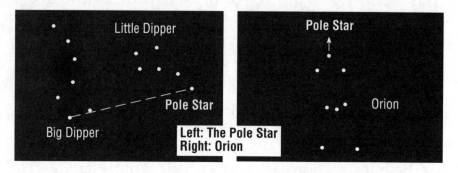

Left: The Pole Star
Right: Orion

Using your thumb and middle finger, measure the distance between the pointers. Then take four "steps" the size of this distance with your fingers in the direction shown. This will lead you to the Pole Star which is at the end of the Little Dipper.

Orion

Orion is another star group which can lead you to the North Star. Known as the giant of the sky, Orion's stars look like the shape of a man. Made up of eight stars, Orion's Head (a small star) points to the Pole Star. The three small stars making up Orion's Belt are extra shiny.

QUIZ – SECOND TWENTY

1 How many noughts do you write in the number one million?
2 How long does it take for the earth to rotate around the sun?
3 In 1886 France gave the USA a rather large gift – what was it?
4 What name is given to a clock which works by the sun's shadow moving across its face?
5 In what city is the Eiffel Tower?
6 Who invented the telephone?
7 Who wrote *Charlie and The Chocolate Factory*?
8 If you are facing south-west, what direction is behind you?
9 What famous German composer was deaf?
10 What three-lettered initials give the proper name for a computer screen?
11 What is the emergency telephone number for Fire, Gardaí or Ambulance?
12 Name the Irish swimmer who won three golds and a bronze in the 1996 Olympic Games.
13 Which Asian country has sumo wrestling as its national sport?
14 A doe is a female of which animal?
15 How many squares on a draughtsboard?
16 Where is the Southern Cross?
17 Who are the All-Blacks?

25

18 What does UFO stand for?
19 Which county, on car registration plates, is represented by the letters KE?
20 Does a Bombay Duck walk or fly?

PHOTOGRAPHY

Your first camera should be a simple one. With it you can learn how to take good pictures without having to fiddle with buttons and knobs.

Many tribes of people, for example the American Indian, used to believe that a camera stole their soul and captured it in a little box. Photography is somewhat more scientific than that.

The film in your camera is a roll of paper which has been "painted" with chemicals. These chemicals change when light shines on them. The shapes and colours in front of the camera are then "captured" with these chemical changes.

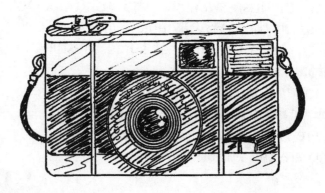

With no film in your camera, remove the lid and look into it. When you click it, a flash of light can be seen. This flash usually lasts about 1/60th of a second. That is enough time for the colours and shapes to be transferred onto a film in the camera. More light will spoil any pictures already taken.

Outdoor photographs are best taken with the sun shining from behind you on to the person or scene to be photographed. People are the best subjects, as long as they don't look at the camera. Looking slightly away will mean the sun does not shine in their eyes – causing them to squint and make funny faces. Worse still, people may sneeze or put a hand in front of their face to shade their eyes.

When taking pictures, hold the camera steady. Make sure your subject is standing still. This should stop "blurring". Ensure the sun is either behind you or to one side. Do not take a picture with the sun shining into your camera. This may result in blank photos due to too much light getting at your film.

Be careful not to let your fingers, camera

straps or anything else get in front of the camera lens. It can be embarrassing to have only a roll of holiday snaps of your fingers to show your friends.

Photographer

In bad light or for indoor photographs, you must use a flash if there is one on your camera. You may need to change the shutter speed when using a flash. Check this in the manual that comes with your camera.

These are only basic hints. Remembering them should mean that you get good, clear photos taken with your simple camera.

THE BEAUFORT SCALE

During a weather forecast you may hear something like "There will be rain with wind speeds, force six to gale force eight." These numbers may mean nothing to you now but if you intend going camping they may be very important.

Number	Description	Speed	Visible Effects
0	Calm	2 Km/H	No wind, smoke rises vertically.
1	Light air	4 Km/H	Smoke blows, wind vanes do
			not move.
2	Light breeze	10 Km/H	Leaves on trees and wind
			vanes move.
3	Gentle breeze	17 Km/H	Light flags will wave.
4	Moderate breeze	22 Km/H	Dust, papers and twigs move.
5	Fresh breeze	35 Km/H	Small trees bend.
6	Strong breeze	45 Km/H	Umbrellas hard to use.
7	Moderate gale	55 Km/H	Trees move, walking difficult.
8	Fresh gale	70 Km/H	Trees lose twigs, walking
			very difficult.
9	Strong gale	80 Km/H	Chimneys and slates blown
			from houses.
10	Whole gale	90 Km/H	Trees uprooted. Buildings damaged.
11	Storm	100 Km/H	Buildings badly damaged.

PLACES TO VISIT WITH YOUR CUB PACK

The scout den is the centre of activity for most cub packs. It's there cubs meet each other for the first time and carry out most of their training. We all know how good it is to get away from the ordinary things we do once in a while. Cubs and leaders benefit greatly from a day's activity in a new setting. Here are a few ideas of places you could go with your cub friends.

The Baily Lighthouse – Howth, Co Dublin.
Lighthouse Heritage Centre – Cork.
Funderland – Visits Irish venues at Christmas and New Year.
Fire Stations – Can be arranged with your local fire chief.
Youth Hostels – Nationwide. An Óige, the Irish Youth Hostel Association, has some fifty houses throughout Ireland. These are mostly in scenic, wooded areas ideal for hiking bases. A Y.H.A. leader's card will allow cub leaders to bring a group of cubs hostelling.
Saltee Islands – Three miles off the coast of Kilmore Quay, Co Wexford. The Saltee Islands are Ireland's largest bird sanctuary. Seals and dolphins also seek refuge on these uninhabited islands.
King John's Castle – Limerick. Enjoy an audio-visual journey from the 13th century, including models and 3D displays. See weapons which were used before gunpowder or patriot missiles. Magnificent view of Limerick city and river Shannon from the towers and battlements.
Fota Wildlife Park – Cork. See giraffes, flamingos, antelopes, ostriches and other animals roam around this forty-acre park.
Salthill Leisure Complex – Galway.

Dublinia Exhibition – Dublin. See Dublin as it was from the Norman landing of 1170 to 1540. Your electronic guide in one of five languages introduces lifesize scenes and scale models. Enjoy an audio-visual show and end with a view of Dublin from St. Michael's Tower.

Blarney Castle – Cork. Famous for its Blarney Stone, said to make great speakers of those who kiss it. Built in the mid-15th century it was owned by the McCarthys. When the Earl of Leicester failed to capture it he sent confusing reports to Queen Elizabeth I. These were referred to as being "all blarney", a term still used to describe cajoling talk.

Seaside Holiday Resort – Bray, Co Wicklow.

Apart from the above, there are numerous other venues for fun and leisure activities, such as swimming pools, ice skating rinks, museums, cinemas, pantomimes, waxworks, forest and hill walks and bowling alleys.

This is only a short list of the many opportunities for bringing cubs on a day's outing. The possibilities are endless and limited only by the imagination of cubs and their leaders.

PUZZLE PAGES

Being clever and resourceful, cubs love solving puzzles. Here are a few for you which you may like to share with your friends.

Cub Wordsearch

Can you find the following words, used a lot by cubs, in our wordsearch? These words run up, down, forwards, backwards and diagonally anywhere around the frame.

Camping, Log, Rope, Sixer, East, Cub Scout, Lamp,
Baloo, Larchill, Pan, Map, Knot

K	T	E	O	C	S	I	X	E	R
I	O	U	K	N	O	I	R	E	O
L	N	T	O	N	K	O	X	O	P
T	L	A	R	C	H	I	L	L	E
O	A	E	P	L	S	T	S	A	E
U	R	M	K	C	M	B	A	L	B
C	A	M	D	O	A	P	U	N	U
L	O	G	N	I	P	M	A	C	K

Crossword

Across
1 Group of cubs (4)
3 The sun is an early
...... (5)
7 Crawl (5)
8 Motor (6)
10 Money dispensing
machine (3)
12 Foot end (3)
17 Do fish learn here? (6)
20 B.P.'s first post as
officer (5)
21 Co. Clare town (5)
22 Resting place (4)

Down
1 Needly tree (4)

2 Rough rock on
mountain (4)
3 A running
competition (4)
4 Smell (5)
5 Knot only for pulling
(4)
6 Four quarters (3)
9 Squirrel food (3)
11 Rudyard's peacock (3)
13 From early days (5)
14 3-in-1 vaccination (3)
15 Camp centre (4)
16 Final tune (4)
18 Whale of a name (4)
19 Rope circle (4)

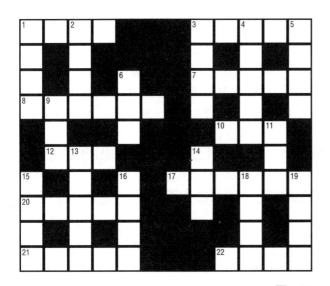

33

Mystery Word
Solve the following three-letter words to read a special word downwards. (They give great support to cubs and scouts!)

___ ___ ___	Fasten a knot
___ ___ ___	Snake-like fish
___ ___ ___	Short sleep
___ ___ ___	Highest part
___ ___ ___	Meat or fruit cooked in pastry
___ ___ ___	Night bird
___ ___ ___	Mouth's edge
___ ___ ___	Chew and swallow
___ ___ ___	Heats the earth

Names Mix–Up
John had no pen to write down the names of places his cub pack would visit. Being a clever scout he decided to use the letters of his Scrabble set. But his small sister upset the table before he could write the place names down on paper. The letters from each place fell beside each other. Can you help John unravel the names? He remembers there are eight counties, two rivers, one province and a harbour on the list.

RAMTIN	WLYAGA	NHASNON	REILSTEN
RYREK	ONETRY	SOLASRER	YEFILF
ALEODNG	THOUL	DOXERWF	LARKEID

Coded Message

The following message is sent to all cub scouts. It is sent in a code which you should try to break in order to read this important note. The key to the code is 1 = A, 2 = B, 3 = C, 4 = D, etc. Can you decode and read it?

1 • 7, 15, 15, 4 • 3, 21, 2 • 19, 3, 15, 21, 20
1, 12, 23, 1, 25, 19 • 4, 15, 5, 19 • 20, 8, 5, 9 18
2, 5, 19, 20.

FIRST AID
....

While in cubs, girls and boys take part in many games and activities. Even with the greatest of care, slight accidents will happen. These may cause some discomfort to the victim. Most minor accidents can be treated with a little common sense, some sympathy and plenty of tact.

When a person cuts their face in an accident, some goose is sure to say, "Oh, you're just pouring blood!" A tactful first-aider will calmly say, "Let's clean your face a little and see what needs to be done." Some people become frightened at the sight and even the thought of blood. People with some training in first aid will not have time to think of the blood. Their only thought will be, "How will I treat this victim to make them safe and comfortable?"

The most important thing that you as a

cub can do is **send someone for adult help.** There are some things though that you can do for the patient until help arrives.

Keep the patient warm by covering him or her with a blanket or jacket. This helps to prevent shock which may cause more harm than the original injury.

The patient should not be given anything to drink unless a medical person says so.

If a crowd of onlookers gathers, get someone to disperse them. People getting "entertainment" at accident scenes block air to the patient, frighten them, or block the way for the ambulance — perhaps all three.

If a person is bleeding you should put a clean cloth, bandage or cotton wool on the cut and press gently. In most cases this will stop the flow of blood. If the bleeding continues you must send for help immediately.

Cuts must be kept clean. This is to prevent germs getting into the wound or bloodstream, causing an infection.

If you suspect that the patient has a broken arm, the arm must be made steady and comfortable. The best way of achieving this is by using a sling to hold it in place. A cub has a ready-made sling – your neckerchief.

A nosebleed can be frightening not only for the patient but also for onlookers. Stay calm! Get the patient to sit upright and pinch the bridge of their nose (just between  the eyes) for a few minutes until the flow stops. If bleeding persists, get adult help.

Bruises and slight swellings (as a result of a fall or knock) may be treated by applying an ice pack – improvise using ice cubes wrapped in a clean cloth.

While it's natural to want to help, there are times when it's best to do nothing. Here are a list of things you must **never** do at the scene of an accident:

1 If you suspect that they've has taken a poisonous substance, do not make the patient vomit. The poison will burn the throat as it comes back up.

2 If you suspect a back injury, do not move the patient and do not allow anyone else to move them either. There is a distinct possibility, in cases of back and neck injuries, that incorrect treatment will lead to paralysis. Get someone to dial 999 immediately.

3 Do not give the patient anything to

eat or drink. This will prevent them from getting an anaesthetic at the hospital, and delay treatment.

4 If the case of a leg injury, make sure that the leg is not broken. Otherwise, do not allow the patient to stand.

5 Do not try to remove sharp objects (glass, knife, stone, etc) which are embedded in the patient's flesh.

Remember, it's just as important to mind yourself!

- Beware of traffic on roads.
- Take great care in electric shock cases — switch off power first and foremost.
- In cases of a gas leakage, switch off gas, open windows — do not turn on electrical switches or light a match.
- Be sensible and calm, otherwise the ambulance people will have a second casualty when they arrive — you!

First Aider

A Basic First Aid Kit Should Contain

A Triangular Bandage	Plastic Gloves
Antiseptic Cream	Paracetemol *
Thermometer	Cough Medicine *
Tweezers	Indigestion Tablets *
Scissors	Mild Laxative *
Packet of Assorted Plasters	Calamine Lotion *
	Three Roller Bandages
Safety Pins	Packet of Cotton Wool

* Must only be used by a trained adult

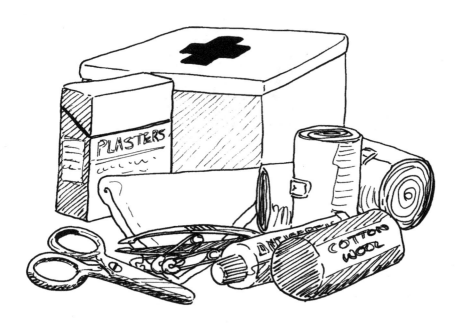

SCIENCE
· · · · · · · · · · · · · · ·

Many people think of science as a topic they could not possibly deal with. Cubs makes this a fun subject by showing how ordinary things work. This is done by playing and learning at the same time. The Scientist Badge introduces four branches of science: chemistry, physics, electricity and biology.

Scientist

CHEMISTRY
· ·

Invisible Ink
Long ago writing was the only way to send messages over long distances. People used a lot of tricks to protect their secrets from busybodies. A favourite way was to send a letter containing ordinary news with one side seeming blank. The person receiving the letter

would wait until they were alone then hold the letter near a lighted candle. As if by magic a written message would appear on the empty page. It would look as if it was written in brown ink. Here's how to do it.

Put some lemon juice on a saucer. Using a dip pen, or something similar, dip it in the lemon juice and write your name on a piece of paper. You will have to look carefully to see the traces of lemon juice in which your name is written. After a few minutes even this faint marking will disappear.

Even though it cannot be seen, a trail of citric acid from the lemon juice is still on the paper. Hold the paper close to a heat source, for example, a light bulb or a candle. The trail of your name will change colour and be seen as brown ink.

PHYSICS

Magnets
These are pieces of metal which attract other metals. They usually come in one of two shapes, the bar magnet or the horseshoe magnet.

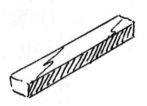
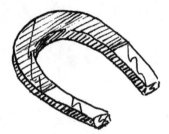

Making A Compass
Place a bar magnet on a small piece of wood. Then put this in a dish of water, so that it floats freely. The magnet and float will turn around until the magnet points a certain way. Gently spin the float and leave it to settle again. It will point the same way.

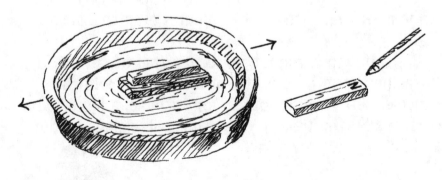

Using a compass you will notice that one end of the magnet points north while the other end points south. Mark "N" on the end pointing north, using a felt pen. Then get another bar magnet and do the same. Mark ".N" on the north-pointing end of the second magnet also.

Now hold your two magnets close to each other. If you hold the two "N" ends near each other they will jump away. The same happens if you hold the two south-pointing ends together. However, the north and the south ends will jump together if brought close.

This magnetic principle "Unlike Poles Attract, Like Poles Repel" is the basis of the electric motor. Can you guess what small magnet scouts should carry in their pocket when hiking? Yes, it is the needle in their compass.

ELECTRICITY

The Electric Light

Did you ever wonder how your torch works? The electricity in the battery flows when you switch on the torch. This flow goes into the bulb, causing it to heat. A fine wire in the bulb glows white hot. This glow is magnified by the bulb glass. The light is made into a strong beam by the mirror or lens around the bulb.

You can make an electric battery light with a few cheap parts. You will need:

- A four and a half volt battery.

- Three pieces of wire about six inches long.
- A screw-in six volt bulb.
- A holder for the bulb, i.e. a plastic bulb holder.
- Connect these as shown below. When you touch wires 2 and 3 together the electricity flows from the battery through the bulb and back to the battery again. If the wire connection is broken anywhere the flow stops. A switch will break the connection just like parting the wires. In a torch the metal body takes the place of the wires.

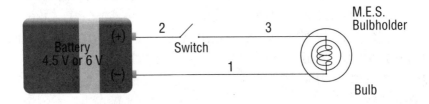

The electric light

BIOLOGY

Pulse and Breathing

People breathe at about 12 breaths per minute when they are resting. After exercise, such as running, this will increase, perhaps to as much as 24 breaths per minute. This is what we call panting. The air we breathe contains oxygen which is needed to freshen our blood.

Our heart pumps the blood around our bodies. The heart beats about 72 times per minute. After exercise this will increase, carrying extra oxygen through our bodies to help us recover. The heart rate can be measured by feeling the pulse at the wrist as shown. Your cub leader will show you how to do this.

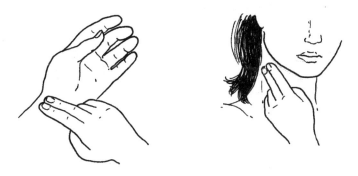

Compare "resting" pulse rates and respiration with "exercise" pulse rates. Measure three cubs' pulse rates and listen to their breathing. Write these down. Have the cubs do about four minutes skipping, running or other exercise. Measure again their pulses and the number of breaths they take per minute. The second set of measurements will be greater than the first as their bodies recover from the exercise. The difference between the first and second measurement for each person can be an indication for how fit the person is.

45

QUIZ – THIRD TWENTY

1 Where is Áras an Uachtaráin?
2 Name the footbridge across the Liffey between O'Connell Bridge and Capel Street Bridge.
3 The Silver Shadow is a model of which famous car?
4 In which county is the town of Mullingar?
5 On a map scaled at a half-inch to one mile, what distance is represented by three inches?
6 Name the three arrows which cubs may be awarded.
7 What date is St. Patrick's Day?
8 Where is the nearest public phone to this scout den?
9 Write S.O.S. in Morse code.
10 When you mix blue and green paint what colour do you get?
11 What picture is opposite the harp on a 5p coin?
12 In what direction from Ireland is Spain?
13 What do you call the part of a camera which opens and closes as you take a picture?
14 What is the title of the Irish National Anthem?
15 Name a word beginning with "J" which means a large gathering of scouts.
16 What is the capital of France?
17 In what year was the battle of Clontarf?
18 In what country is the Leaning Tower of Pisa?
19 What tree is grown from acorns?
20 Which fish did Fionn Mac Cumhail eat to gain his great knowledge?

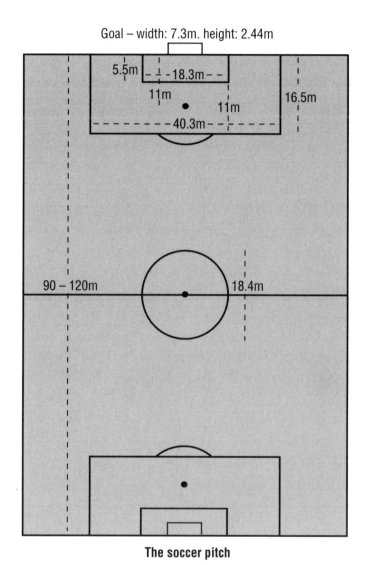

Goal – width: 7.3m. height: 2.44m

5.5m

- -18.3m- -

11m

11m

16.5m

- - - - - - - - -40.3m- - -

90 – 120m

18.4m

The soccer pitch

Goal – width: 6.5m. height: 2.5m (uprights: 7m)

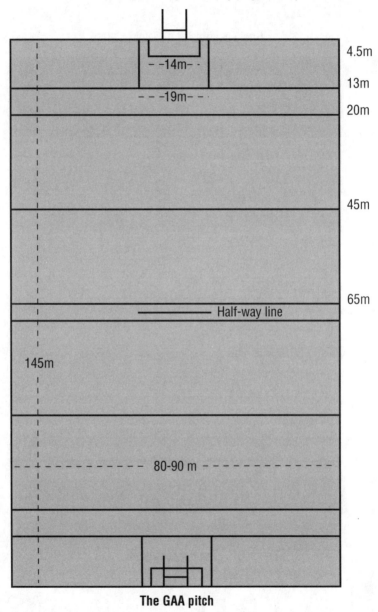

4.5m

- - -14m- - -

13m

- - -19m- - ·

20m

45m

65m

Half-way line

145m

80-90 m

The GAA pitch

SPORTS BADGE

To gain the Sports badge a cub should have a good knowledge of some sports activities. This usually includes the rules of different sports. Young Irish people have a great interest in Gaelic football, hurling and soccer. The measurements of the playing fields for these games are important. However, this information can be hard to come by. In the previous two pages you can clearly see and study diagrams and measurements for these particular playing fields.

Sports

GOLD ISLAND

Short Jim Copper and his band of sixty-five year old pirates have returned to Gold Island. They are here to dig up the treasure they buried thirty-five years ago for their retirement. Not being very good pirates they drank too much rum and now feel sick. They have all fallen asleep and left their map on the sand. Can you find the treasure before they wake up?

The map scale is 1 centimetre of parchment = 1 km of island.

To find riches beyond your wildest dreams,
Follow these steps, it's not where it seems.
Start at the bottom of Crow's Nest Ridge.
Walk 8 kms west, then 1/2 km south.
Go next 1 km northwest and 1 km northeast.
Now travel 1/2 km south, finally 8 kms east.
Observe closely the track you made,
To see where to struggle with pick and spade.

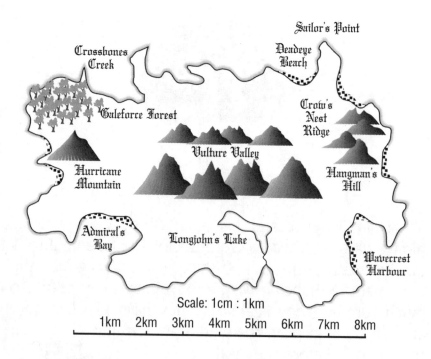

Sailor's Point

Crossbones Creek

Deadeye Beach

Galeforce Forest

Crow's Nest Ridge

Vulture Valley

Hurricane Mountain

Hangman's Hill

Admiral's Bay

Longjohn's Lake

Wavecrest Harbour

Scale: 1cm : 1km

1km   2km   3km   4km   5km   6km   7km   8km

DANGER! ELM TREE

"We are twenty-two cubs and four cub scouters,
Happy to be hiking in the big bright outdoors."

The cheerful chant of twenty-two young voices rang through the woods. Whit weekend was a great time for camping, with clear weather and a fresh breeze.

The group headed slowly but surely for their camping spot in the Wicklow mountains. Some of the younger boys and girls felt tired. These were cheered on and made feel strong by encouraging words from the leaders and older cubs.

"We're almost at the campsite now," James announced.

"Just another twenty minutes or so," Joan added.

The two leading adults would be glad to reach the campsite. Paul and Ann were behind the group, keeping an eye on the slower ones and calling for the pack to slow down if those at the front were moving too fast.

A group of teenagers appeared from the woods. "Aw, look at them all with their big bags and tents," one of the teenagers said. "Yeah," said another, "you'd think they were going to the North Pole." The cubs and their leaders ignored these remarks and saved their energy for walking. The youths realised their taunts were not bothering the cub pack and ran off in front of the young scouts.

When the cubs arrived at the clearing they intended using for their campsite, the youths were already there, sitting around a radio playing loud music. When they saw the cub pack they began to jeer again. "We got here before yez!" they chanted childishly.

The four leaders gathered the cubs in a corner of the clearing. After a quick chat Paul left his rucksack with the group and did a quick scout around the area. He found another clearing about ten minutes walk away and returned to the pack. "We hadn't noticed that camping spot when we checked this place two weeks ago," he said. "Luckily it seems better suited for camping than this one."

As the cubs prepared for another short walk Joan noticed the youths had very little equipment or food for camping. She was concerned to see that they had tied a big plastic sheet over an elm tree as a makeshift tent. Joan tried to advise the group about the danger of using the elm in that way, since they are not strong trees. They only scoffed at her, saying she was just jealous of their good camping spot. Then they rudely turned their radio up to drown out any advice the cub leaders wished to offer. "Come on," Ann said, "we're just wasting our breath."

After their short rest the cubs were able for another short walk. Soon they arrived at the campsite Paul had found. The happy group then worked together erecting three tents.

The leaders' tent went in the middle. It had two rooms, one for Paul and James, the other for Ann and Joan. The leaders and cubs worked as a team. Finally the cubs hammered in the tent pegs which the adults had carefully placed in their correct positions.

Soon the smell of soup, sausages and beans drifted to the noses of the hungry cubs. They gathered firewood with Paul and Ann, while James and Joan cooked the meal. Paul and Ann explained to the cubs which branches and twigs to gather from the ground. Some trees are unsuitable for firewood, they told them.

"The poplar and willow trees give very little heat," Ann explained.

"And the elder tree has a bitter smelling smoke," added Paul.

At last the food was ready for eating. The hungry pack sat around the campfire and chatted merrily about the day's excitement. The four leaders made final plans for the evening game.

Meanwhile the group of youths were having trouble. They had very little food with them as each thought the others would bring enough for two. The food they had was spoilt when it fell in the fire they lit. This fire gave off a smelly smoke because they were burning the wrong trees. Worst of all, their radio had stopped working because the batteries had run down and they had no spares. In other words, they were not prepared because they had not planned in advance.

After their meal, the cub group washed their dishes and pots with water from the nearby stream. An exciting game of Fetch the Flag was organised by the leaders and enjoyed by all. When the game finished a sing-song was held around the camp fire. This was finished with the scout taps and

53

the tired pack of cubs went to bed.

As always, two of the leaders went to sleep while the other two remained awake to mind the cubs. James and Ann took first watch. The excited chatter from the two tents of cubs soon faded away. The girls and boys, tired from their hiking and games, soon fell asleep

After a couple of hour's sleep Joan and Paul rose to keep watch. As the four leaders sat in the still, fresh spring air they listened to the sounds of the night. The quiet stillness was occasionally broken by the call of a woodland animal or the gentle rustle of leaves in the night. The sweet scent of trees and plants wafted through the air bringing a fresh fragrance to their nostrils.

Suddenly the peace was shattered by a loud **crack!** This was followed by frightened shouts and screams. The four leaders jumped up from their tree stump seats. "Something's happened to that group of teenagers!" Paul said. "Ann and I will stay here, while you and James go see what's wrong." Joan responded.

The two men hurried towards the shouting voices. When they reached the other clearing they saw that the elm tree had fallen. The makeshift tent was a crumpled mess. Two of the youths were scrambling around in the tree branches, shouting. Two others were standing like statues, as white as ghosts, helpless with shock. "Help us, please!" one of the girls said. "Jimmy and Mick are trapped." "I think Jimmy is hurt bad," said one of the boys.

The two scouters, being trained first-aiders, looked

quickly and carefully at the situation. Paul told one of the youths to run to the campsite and return with Joan and two cubs. "We also need our bush saw and axes," he instructed. Meanwhile Paul and James began to work at rescuing the two trapped youths.

One of the teenagers was yelling in panic. The other was quiet, too quiet, James thought. Paul spoke calmly to the frightened young lad. "Listen, your friend is badly hurt," he said. "If you remain cool we can help you both." "OK," the lad replied, "but I'm scared." Paul and James examined the fallen tree.

"It looks bad," James said. "If the tree moves too much it may crash down on the tent completely."

"Yes," replied Paul, "we need more expert help for rescuing the unconscious lad."

Joan arrived with Peter and Mary, two ten year old cubs. Joan said some of the cubs back at camp were scared. Ann was being helped by the older cubs to keep them happy with a sing-song. Some of the older cubs were making soup and the teenagers could have some when it was ready.

The four frightened teenagers who were not in the tent were brought back to the campsite and given soup. "I hope Mick and Jimmy will be OK," one said. Ann tried to console them as she dished out the soup. "Our scouts will help them," she replied, "and we can get help here soon from more experienced people."

Meanwhile, back at the fallen elm tree the group were discussing plans. "Paul and I will remain here cutting carefully at the tree while you go for help with young Peter and Mary," James said to Joan.

Joan took the orienteer's map from her pocket. She pointed it using her compass. Then studying it carefully she saw a farmhouse marked on it. Looking down the hill in the direction indicated by the map the lights of this house could be seen. It was about two miles away to the northwest. "We can reach that house in about forty minutes," Joan said. "Be careful," Paul warned, "we don't want any more casualties."

The trio set off down the hill. Each carried a torch and whistle in case they got parted in the darkness. There were slippery slopes and small ledges to be overcome. They helped each other over the rough ground. "Now I know why we were told to wear flat shoes with good sole grips," Peter said. "Yes," replied Mary, "my slippy high heels would be no good on this sort of ground."

"That's right," Joan told them. "There's a good reason for everything you are told to do in cubs."

The going got rough as they went down the hill towards the farmhouse. At times they would lose sight of the farmhouse as they went down behind a hill. Then they would use their compass and map to keep on the right track. "Now I'm really glad I did my Pathfinder's Badge," Peter said.

Suddenly Joan shouted, "Help! I'm falling!" Mary and Peter grabbed her, saving her from a nasty trip.

"Joan tripped over a plastic bag, left on the ground

by some untidy hikers," Mary said crossly.

"Some people never learn," said Peter. "All they had to do was roll it up and put it in their pocket like this." He stuffed the offending bag in his pocket so that it would cause no more harm.

Then he saw it. "Oh-oh, our compass won't point north now," he said softly. As he shone his torch on the ground Joan and Mary saw the broken compass.

"Oh, I'm sorry," Joan said. "I dropped it as I was falling."

"Don't worry," young Mary said, "between us we should remember how to find the North Star."

"Very clever," said Peter. "I know that the two stars at the end of the Big Dipper point towards it."

"Yes," Mary said excitedly, "and Orion's head points to it too."

The three hikers looked upwards, searching the star-filled sky. "Look," Peter said, pointing, "there's the Big Dipper."

"Well done!" Joan responded. "Now find its base and follow four times the distance between the last two stars."

"I see Orion!" Mary said. "I can make out his shiny belt. Now I see his head, and the next star is the North Star."

Just to be on the safe side, Joan checked for the Little Dipper. Finding it, she agreed its tail was the same star which the others decided was the North Star. "Well done!" Joan cried. "Now facing north, we know north-west is forty-five degrees to our left."

"It must be over that little hill," Peter said pointing.

When they reached the hilltop the lights of the house were only a short distance away. Minutes later they were telling their story to the people who lived there. The woman of the house telephoned the Gardaí while the man made tea and sandwiches for the tired, hungry hikers.

"The mountain rescue team are on the way," the woman said when she came into the room. "It won't take long — they're coming by helicopter."

"Thank goodness," Joan sighed. "I think they'll need to hurry."

"If we could let your friends know it would give them a boost," the man of the house said. "There are no roads up to them and by the time we could reach them by foot help will have arrived," he continued.

"I have an idea," said Mary.

Back at the campsite, Paul and James were working hard. "Now that we've freed one of the lads we must concentrate on keeping the tree from falling on the other," Paul said.

"We have it shored up well," James replied, "but the sooner help arrives the better."

"Not knowing how Joan and the two cubs are doing is bothering me," James commented.

At their tent Ann and the cubs were thinking the same. They were busy helping the injured teenager as well as the other three. However, they were also concerned for their friends who had gone for help in the dark. They sometimes looked towards the distant lights of the farmhouse. "Hey, the lights are flashing," a cub said excitedly. "That's morse code," said another, "Mary and I learned it for our Communicator's Badge."

"Quickly – get a pen and paper and write down what you can," Ann said to the badge-winning cub.

The cub wrote:

X./O/T H/E/R/E O/K C/O/X/T/E/R
X./O/I/N/X. T/O X/O/U

"They keep sending that," he reported. "I know most of it. The Xs I don't know and the three Xs with dots are the same."

Another cub said, "Let me see, I'm good at crosswords." She looked at the paper and thought carefully. After a while she said, "The Xs with dots are Gs, so it says GOT HERE OK CO/X/TER GOING TO X/OU. The last word is YOU."

"And the other word is COPTER for helicopter," said another cub. "So the message says, GOT HERE OK COPTER GOING TO YOU!"

"Hooray!" cheered the cubs. "Let's go tell Paul and James."

The two men were relieved to hear the news.

Twenty minutes later the helicopter arrived. It landed two fields away so as not to shake the elm tree. The rescue team freed the boy from the tree. A doctor then treated him and he was stretchered to the waiting helicopter.

"These young people can be thankful that you cubs were around tonight," the doctor said. "Without your help that lad might not have survived."

"Will he be all right?" James asked.

"He'll be fine now that we have him in our care," the doctor replied.

Some weeks later the cub pack had six visitors to their den. It was the teenagers to say thank you. They realised how silly they had been for jeering the brave, helpful, cheerful bunch of cubs who helped them so much.

HOW TO MAKE A LOG LAMP

When camping or youth hostelling darkness comes too quickly for some cubs. There are always those who would like to read a little longer, although cubs must listen to their leaders when told to turn out their light.

Using a torch may help you to read. The trouble is you must hold a torch with one hand and you need two hands to hold a book in bed. No need to grow a third hand, though – you can make a bedside lamp with a little help from an adult.

First, get a small log about ten inches long and six inches in diameter. Now find a helpful adult. Better still, get together with a few cub friends and a cub leader to make one lamp each.

Ask the adult to help you cut a straight base on the log. This is to ensure that the log will stand on its end.

The log should now be about nine inches long. Next, cut two inches off each end of your log, (i) and (ii). This gives you a log of about five inches long by six inches in diameter. Your adult friend will help you cut a "V" shape in your log as shown in (ii). and drill a small hole (about 1/4 inch) through the back of your log.

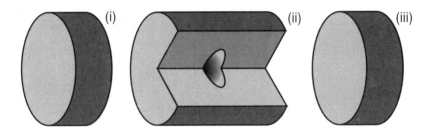

Now apply a couple of coats of varnish to the inside of the "V" and to both sides of the two discs you cut from the ends of your log. You should also varnish both ends of the log. Allow time to dry. While waiting you should assemble the electric lamp in the Science section (page 43–44). After testing the lamp, disassemble, leaving the two leads connected to the bulb holder.

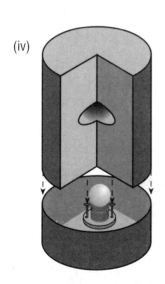

Carefully hold the log on the base disc. Keep the lamp

holder in position as in (iv). When you are satisfied the holder is centred in the "V", mark its position on the base. Put the log to one side and screw the lamp holder in position on the base. Then using wood-glue stick the log to the base so the lamp holder is in the middle of the "V". Allow the glue to set — this may take some hours.

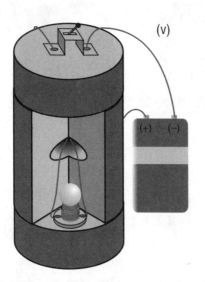

Bring the two leads from the lamp through the hole in the log. Again, using wood-glue, cement the top disc to the log and allow to set. You can now complete the assembly of the light with switch and battery. The switch can be glued or screwed to the top of your log as in (v). Small switches, which look good on this lamp, can be bought in electrical shops.

The complete unit should give you many hours of light. Why not make some for presents or for selling at your annual scout fund-raising fair!

SMILE A WHILE

Cubs are humorous, fun-loving people. During hikes and at night beside the camp fire you will always have a session of jokes. Here are a few to bring a cheerful smile to the faces of your friends.

What did the man say when he walked into the bar?
Ouch!

Listening to my sister playing the violin, you would think the strings were still in the cat.

Patient: "Doctor, doctor. People keep ignoring me!"
Doctor: "Next please!"

Patient: "Doctor, doctor, I keep thinking I'm a pack of cards."
Doctor: "Sit over there, I'll deal with you in a minute."

Did you hear about the silly sea scout?
His tent sank!

Patient: "Doctor, doctor, what should I do with a broken ankle?"
Doctor: "Limp!"

Patient: "Doctor, doctor, I keep thinking I'm a pair of curtains!"
Doctor: "Well, just pull yourself together."

The door of an aeroplane carrying Japanese car parts burst open while airborne. As its contents fell from the sky a little boy was heard shout, "Look, Mammy, it's raining Datsun cogs!"

Patient: "Doctor, doctor, I keep thinking that I'm a dog."
Doctor: "How long have you had this problem?"
Patient: "Ever since I was a little pup."

Patient: "Doctor, doctor, I can't stop stealing."
Doctor: "I'll just give you something to take."

Patient: "Doctor doctor, I keep thinking I'm invisible!"
Doctor: "I can't see you now."

Knock knock.
Who's there?
Amos.
Amos who?
A mosquito bit me.

Knock knock.
Who's there?
Andy.
Andy who?
Andy bit me again.

Knock knock.
Who's there?
Tyrone.
Tyrone who?
Tyrone shoe lace!

Knock knock.
Who's there?
Felix.
Felix who?
Felix my ice cream again I'll belt him!

CUB GAMES
·······················

Whether at camp or back home at the den, good weather or bad, cub scouting presents a host of opportunities for fun and games – and for healthy team spirit. The following pages suggest and explain a number of games that can be played in different weathers and surroundings.

Fetch The Flag

Divide the cubs into two equal teams. Two flags (different coloured pieces of cloth) are tied to sticks which are then stuck in the ground with a two foot square drawn around them. These areas should be about forty feet apart. Mark a circle about six feet in diameter, at least ten feet away from each flag area. These are jails owned by the team near the flags. Then mark a halfway line between the flags.

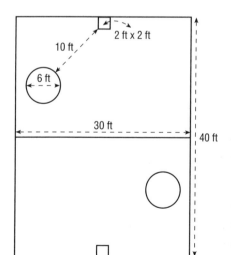

The purpose of the game is to capture the other team's flag without getting caught yourself. The opposition's flag must be brought to your own flag place and must touch the ground on the square.

65

It must not be thrown but touched down, rugby style.

The game is started with each team in its own jail circle. At a signal, e.g. whistle blow, both teams attempt to capture the other flag. As soon as a player crosses into the other team's half, he/she may be caught by touching, and brought to jail.

If a player is caught with the opposition's flag in his/her hand the flag is returned to base. A player may pass the flag to a member of his or her own team. It must be handed, not thrown.

A jailed player may be released by one of their own team running in to the jail and shouting "I release you!" Everybody in jail at this time is freed to rejoin the game. They can be re-captured immediately by touching.

Boundaries must be set and kept to by the players. The drawing on page 65 shows the game layout. The size of play area may be altered to suit the players. Trees and bushes may be included for hidey places, but all players must remain in the play area. Any player going outside this must go to jail immediately.

String–A-Long

This is an ideal game for playing in the woods. You will need lots of string or wool – about fifteen feet for every two cubs. If you have twenty cubs you will need ten fifteen foot lengths. You also require a pen and a piece of paper for each cub.

String the wool around the trees, gates, posts, bushes or any obstacles you can find. Do not tie it, just loop it. Cross the lengths over each other for more fun. Then write each cub's name on an end of wool. The cubs must find their end, unravel the string and roll it up on a stick which you provide. The papers with initials must be returned with the string. To avoid disagreements you should keep a note of the pairs you make as you lay the trails.

The first pair to return everything neatly to the leaders wins. This includes an unbroken fifteen foot length of string.

Push–A–Block

This game may be played in the den. You need two long-handled brushes or brooms, and two blocks of wood.

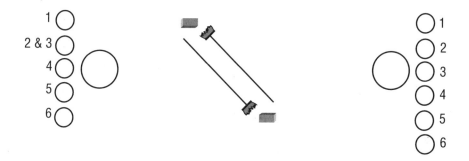

Mark a circle about one foot in diameter with chalk, near opposite walls.

Make teams of players, using your sixes. Line up the teams, as shown, with the most athletic cubs on each team given number ones. Try to equalise cubs with the same number. If sixes have unequal numbers present this can be overcome by giving

67

players on the smaller team two numbers.

Place the two brushes halfway between teams, as shown. A leader then calls out a number at random. The two cubs with this number run to the centre, grab a brush and use it to sweep the block from one circle to the circle near his/her own team. One point is scored for each race won. When all cubs have had their turn count the scores.

Good Knights

This game enacts the jousting sessions of knights of yore without causing the same amount of harm!

You will need a potato, a tablespoon and a stick about one foot long (the sticks will only be needed for half the members of each team).

Teams split into horses and knights. The cubs playing the horses go on their hands and knees. The knights sit on their backs. Knights hold the potato on the spoon while holding their sword (stick) in the other hand.

One duo at a time do battle with each other, trying to knock their opponent's potato. The first to do so without losing their own is the winner. If both knights lose their potato together the contest is a draw.

This can become a competition between sixes with points gained for each win.

Time To Go

The only equipment for this game is a watch. It may be played outdoors or indoors.

Use chairs, chalk marks, ropes, etc, to indicate start and finish lines about fifty feet apart. In groups of ten or twelve the cubs line up at the start. The leader gives a signal to begin and the cubs start walking towards the finish line. The idea is to get to the finish in exactly one minute (without looking at a watch or clock). The player or team of players must begin walking and not stop until they reach the finish line. Of course, players may speed up or slow down their walk as they go.

Crab Football

Most young people enjoy a game of football, but with the limits of your average scout den, normal football would mean spending a fortune on glass panes. However, a solution is to hand! The game of crab football now means that, good weather or bad, an energetic, fun-filled game is always possible.

Cubs are divided into teams with about five or six players on each side. Wooden benches are laid down at either end of the room for goals. The ball must strike the seat of the bench, and not go past or over it, to score.

The players must get into a crab-like position. They sit on the floor and place their hands on the floor behind them. They now move around the floor on their hands and feet. The ball may only be kicked with the feet. Touching it with your hands results in a free kick for the opposition.

The ball must remain on the floor at all times. Kicking it off the ground results in a free kick for the opposition.

Care must be taken by the referee cub leader to make sure that there is no dangerous play or rough behaviour. Breaking of rules may lead to a player being sidelined for two or three minutes.

Each team has a goalkeeper who plays kneeling upright. Goalies may handle the ball — but only within a three metre distance of the goal. Chalk lines would obviously be necessary.

A watch and a whistle are required by the referee. Games usually last about ten or fifteen minutes. They may be played on a league basis, or the winner stays on the floor. This is a reliable warm-up game for winter evenings and all cubs can be given a couple of games in a forty-minute period.

SWIMMING SAFELY

Every year there are reports of people drowning while on holiday or even in their local swimming pool. As cubs go on camp their parents or guardians are given a form on which they fill in details of their child's ability to swim. This information makes it easier for the leaders to take care of their young charges.

When cubs are camping near water or partaking in water activities, a person or persons with the group **must** have qualifications in Life Saving and in Artificial Resuscitation. These qualifications must be renewed every three years.

While leaders give great time and effort to ensuring the safety of cubs, there are certain things **all** cubs can do to help.

1 Ensure, where possible, that there is a lifeguard on duty. This is signalled by a red and yellow flag flying from a pole.

2 Never swim alone — use the buddy system. This is where at least two swimmers stay together at all times and protect each other.

3 Ensure ring buoys are available and in good condition.

4 After eating stay out of the water for at least an hour. Your meal must be digested properly. Failure to heed this will possibly cause you to get cramps. Your arms and legs become painful so that it is impossible to swim.

5 When in the sea, swim parallel to the shore and remain within your depth. You get just as wet and can swim just as far without risking your life.

6 Never horse around when swimming either in the sea or in a pool. Rough play can be dangerous and sometimes fatal.

7 Never pretend you are in trouble while swimming. You may distract lifeguards, causing them to miss somebody in real trouble. You may also endanger the lives of your friends or relatives who will go to your rescue.

A visit to the sea or swimming pool can be great fun. A certain amount of splashing and playing is normal behaviour for boys and girls of cub age. Be considerate of your friends who may be non-swimmers or afraid in the water.

Cubs are encouraged to learn to swim with the Swimmer badge being awarded in three stages. The most difficult of these include swimming with clothes on and undressing in the water. This will prepare girls and boys in case they accidentally fall into deep water.

If you are of cub age **do not** go in the water to help someone in trouble. Send someone for help and throw a rope or float to the person. Look for a life buoy if you are on a beach or at a river bank.

Swimmer

COLLECTING

For as long as anyone can remember, people have been collecting things. People take great joy in showing their collections to others. They also get a great deal of

pleasure from looking at another person's collection. Collections may range from aeroplanes to zebras. People collect steam trains, sharks, snakes and all sorts of things!

But there are lots of easier and more available things to collect. Two of the most popular collectibles are stamps and keyrings.

Stamps

A stamp collector is called a philatelist. Stamp collecting can be fun. The stamps are kept in albums. Your first stamp album will probably be a World Stamp Album. This is arranged with the pages marked by countries of the world in alphabetical order. The first country may be Afghanistan and the last may be Zimbabwe.

You can fill this album with stamps given to you by friends and relations. Other stamp collectors will want to swap with you. This gives you a chance to trade stamps you have for those you don't have. There are clubs for stamp collectors. The Irish post office has a special department which helps people who collect stamps. After some years you may decide to concentrate on certain stamps. Some people collect Irish stamps only, or English or African stamps, for example. Other people collect stamps with trains or special pictures on them. There are people who specialise in collecting triangular stamps.

Whatever their special interest, most people begin with a general countries album, collecting any stamp they can get. Stamps collected

73

over a number of years can sometimes be valuable as there may be some rare finds amongst them.

However, the important thing is to enjoy your collection. This is its greatest value to you, not any monetary value you may gain from it.

By collecting stamps you learn about the countries of the world while having fun. Each nation takes great pride in its stamps; they act as international advertisements for the culture and customs of that country.

Keyrings

A collection of keyrings can be very colourful and entertaining to see. They make ideal souvenirs of a holiday or event. Whether you are a football team supporter or a follower of a pop star there is sure to be a keyring for you.

While on holidays try to buy a couple of keyrings. After a while you will be delighted to review your collection. Swapping them with friends can be fun as you trade stories of where and how you found each one. You can display your collection on a wooden shield. After a while you may need to categorise your keyrings. This can be done by using separate shields for each group. You could separate them by colour, country, shape or any other way you wish.

Whatever you decide to do with your collection, you may be certain that a keyring will always be a useful item to have.

QUIZ – FOURTH TWENTY

1 Name the Irish warrior who lost his strength when he fell from his horse after visiting Tír Na nÓg.
2 What river is Cork built on?
3 What program is on R.T.E. 1 each evening at 6.01?
4 Who wrote *Black Beauty?*
5 What is the main ingredient of candy floss?
6 Where would you go abseiling?
7 What colour is the neutral wire in a three pin plug?
8 What should you not do over spilt milk?

75

9 What is a black widow?
10 What musical instrument is the emblem of Ireland?
11 How many edges are on a cube?
12 Who is Taoiseach of Ireland?
13 Which Zodiac sign is a weighing scales?
14 What shape was King Arthur's Table?
15 What do philatelists collect?
16 How many legs does an insect have?
17 In which county is Ireland's highest mountain?
18 In which county is Foulksrath Castle?
19 Which European country is famous for clogs, tulips and windmills?
20 Is a whale a fish?

THE MORSE CODE

This was invented by a man named Samuel Morse. It was the only way to communicate by radio for many years.

A	•−	J	•−−−	S	•••
B	−•••	K	−•−	T	−
C	−•−•	L	•−••	U	••−
D	−••	M	−−	V	•••−
E	•	N	−•	W	•−−
F	••−•	O	−−−	X	−••−
G	−−•	P	•−−−	y	−•−−
H	••••	Q	−−•−	Z	−−••
I	••	R	•−•		

Due to advances in radio systems it is almost outdated now. However, it can have its uses in some cases.

Morse code can be sent by sound or sight. For example, using a light as in our Elm Tree story. A dot is sent with a short flash of light. A dash is shown with a flash lasting three times as long. The space between dots or dashes of the same letter lasts as long as one dot. Between each letter this space lasts as long as one dash. Spacing between words equals seven dots.

The international call for help is S.O.S. which is simple to remember in morse code.

Write it here: _____

KIM'S GAMES

The best way to improve your performance at anything is by practice. "Practice makes perfect" as the saying goes. This applies to your memory as much as anything else. In school you learn poems and other things by memory. Some young people find this difficult. Cubs have a number of games in which their memories and powers of observation are used. These games are referred to as Kim's games.

Box of Junk
Get a large cardboard box and place anything you can find in it. Typical objects in a scout den are ropes, coins, mugs, spoons, woggles, etc.

You should be able to find at least thirty items to put in your box. Make a list of what you have in the box.

Divide your cubs into teams. Then cover the box with a piece of cloth. Now let each team in turn gather

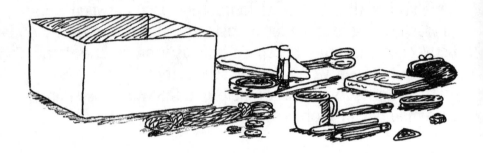

around the box. Uncover the box and let the team look inside for one minute.

After all the teams have viewed the box give each a pen and a sheet of paper. The teams must now write the contents of the box. If there were three pens of different colours the colours must be written down.

Compare the cubs' lists with your complete list.

Two points are scored for each correct item listed.

To prevent guessing you should subtract one point for each wrong item. The team with most points scored is the winner.

Kim's Ear Game

You can check your memory and your sense of hearing with a small change to Kim's game.

As before, fill your box, cover it and let each team

view it in turn. Then hang a sheet in the den or hide from view of the cubs. Drop each object in turn on to the floor or table, ensuring the cubs can't see them. The cubs must write the name of each object in turn, using their memory and ears.

Of course there is no need to say the colour of each pen for this game. However, sharp-eared cubs should be

able to tell the difference between a teaspoon and a dessertspoon.

It's a good idea for the leader to check how easy it is to identify the objects. This can be done by dropping them before any cubs are present.

Kim's Nose Game

This game helps cubs develop a good sense of smell. It sharpens their noses and helps them identify aromas. This is important so that they can realise dangers such as poisonous chemicals, bad food, etc.

Let the cubs see a range of objects on a table. Items such as turf, lemon, candles, coffee, pepper, etc. are ideal. Remove the objects from the table and sit the cubs in a circle on the floor. Blindfold all cubs using their neckerchiefs. For added fairness you

should wrap each item in a clean cloth as you walk around holding them under the cubs' noses.

Keep a note of the order which you "show" the items. When you have given the cubs a smell of all the objects give each team a pen and paper and get them to write the items in the order in which they smelt them.

CAUTION

Items which must **not** be used in this game include glue, turpentine, typing correction fluid and others, which cub leaders should be aware of.

When the teams are writing their answers they should be separated as much as space will allow. A small table should be provided for each team to sit around. Cubs in each team should talk in whispers or write notes to each other so as not to assist opposing teams.

INVERTED PERISCOPE

We have all seen films and documentaries about submarines, but did you know that the periscope used to see what is happening above the water can just as easily be used in reverse?

How many times have you looked into a pond or a stream and not been able to see to the bottom? The water was unclear and blocked your view. Now you can

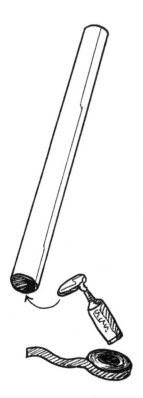

make a reverse periscope to help you look more deeply at the happenings underwater while still staying dry!

You will need about three feet (90 cms) of plastic pipe of 5 inches (12 cms) in diameter, clear perspex cut to the same diameter as the pipe inside (an adult will help you to do this), waterproof glue and a roll of plastic tape approx 2 inches (5 cms) wide.

Apply the glue to the

rim of the perspex. Place the perspex inside the pipe at one end. When the glue has set, cover the outside end of the pipe with plastic tape. Extend the tape over the edge of the pipe by 1 inch (2.5 cms). Apply more waterproof glue around the tape, sealing the perspex to the pipe connection.

Allow plenty of time for the glue to set before using your reverse periscope. Now you can view those underwater plants and fish in spite of any murky water!

Note: Always take great care when around water – you must learn and follow the water safety advice on pages 70–72 at all times.

CYCLING TRIPS

A cub pack may go on short cycling trips once or twice a year. This may be to allow members to achieve their Cyclist's Badge or as part of a cycle hike.

Whatever the purpose, great care must be taken. Listen carefully to your leaders before you start and at all times during your trip.

Before setting out, check the following with an adult: brakes, tyres, steering, chain and gear system. Brake blocks must be in good condition. If worn or uneven they should be replaced before long journeys. Tyres should be checked for cracks in their walls and renewed if damaged. Steering should be smooth and even; loose nuts in the system can cause nasty accidents. The chain should be oiled and rust-free. A good check in a cycle shop costs little compared to the expense of an accident.

Make sure you have front and rear lights when starting out. Even in mid-summer, Irish evenings may become dark and misty due to weather changes. Always have a reflector on your bike rear. These can be put on the front as well. **Reflectors are not a substitute for lights!**

Ensure your bike is the proper size. A bicycle that is too big or too small is difficult to control. If it is too big you will not be able to stop safely. This has been the cause of many cycling accidents.

Check that you know the rules of the road. Special attention should be given to rules for cyclists. Never wear your rucksack when cycling. It will unbalance you, possibly causing you to wobble and crash. Put your tools and equipment in a bag on your carrier.

Always wear a helmet – this is an invaluable and necessary protection should you take a tumble. Only a fool would bang their head on a concrete road when there is a softer option.

While on the road:

1 Listen to, and follow carefully, all instructions from your leader.
2 Keep well to the left.
3 Do not travel three abreast. Keep in a single line if possible.
4 Keep well away from trucks and buses, especially near a corner.
5 Obey all traffic signs – a red light really means stop!
6 Don't weave in and out of slow-moving traffic and never cycle on the footpath.
7 When you break in an emergency, keep your weight on the saddle. Apply the back brake just before the front.
8 Never race on the road. You can **not** watch for cars and trucks when watching other cyclists foolish enough to compete with you.
9 When cycling up a hill it is nice to think of the easy downward slope ahead. You must also consider safety. Do your brakes work? Are all your companions sensible enough to control their bikes on the hill? It's better to walk down very steep hills. The downward slope is more difficult than the uphill climb because it is more dangerous!

Cyclist

In order to earn your Cyclist badge you should also buy and learn to use a puncture repair kit. Keep this kit on your bike at all times.

THE COUNTRY CODE

Of all the joys in being a cub scout, one of the greatest is hiking through green fields and forests. Here you can feel the wind in your hair, smell the fresh country air, see the forty shades of green, hear the birds sing and taste fresh water from a babbling stream.

In order that these wonderful pleasures may be enjoyed for many years to come there are some rules which we should follow. Farmers, foresters and others who depend on the land – this includes **you** who eat food produced there – will be happier, healthier people if we follow the Country Code.

1 **Campfires:** Matches, lighters, etc. must be used with the greatest of care. One single spark has been responsible for destroying forests and crops. Lives have also been lost due to carelessness with fires. Never poke at picnic or campfires. You may cause sparks to jump on dry ground and then WHOOSH! Always ensure campfires are properly put out before leaving the site.

2 **Gates:** When crossing farmland, close all gates properly! Animals can be injured by

85

falling into drains or wandering onto the road. If a gate is open you should close it and, if possible, tell the landowner in case he or she wanted it open.

3 **Streams:** Do not wash dishes or bathe in streams. It is a source of water for many people. If you live in the city you would not like someone to wash their hands in the pot of water you were about to make your tea with.

4 **Litter:** Collect and bring all litter with you. Broken bottles, cans, plastic bags, etc. can harm animals and people using the countryside. It also looks terrible.

5 **Pathways:** When crossing fields you must keep to the pathway. A field of wheat or corn will be destroyed if walked on. This would cost its owner a lot of hardship and money. Even fields of grass must be respected as this is used for hay to feed cattle in winter.

6 **Roads:** When walking or cycling on country roads, keep to the side, preferably in single file but never more than two abreast. Keep behind at least one leader with another at the back of the group. When approaching a bend or corner, stop singing, keep quiet and listen for traffic noises. Be careful on steep hills and when passing cattle or tractors, etc.

THE BOY WHO CRIED WOLF

Long ago, in a small Wicklow village, a young boy named Peter was minding his father's sheep at night.

Some of his father's neighbours had lost sheep to a pack of wolves which were roaming in the area. At first Peter enjoyed being out at night for three hours before his father took over guarding the sheep. After two weeks he had changed his mind.

"This is boring," he thought to himself. "Here I am minding a flock of sheep every night and nothing ever happens." Then he had a very naughty idea. He took a deep breath and shouted, "Wolf!" He yelled again, this time louder than the first. "Wolf! Wolf!" Within minutes his father and some neighbours were racing towards him. "Where is the wolf?" his dad asked, breathless from running across the field.

"Sorry, Dad," Peter said ruefully, "I thought I saw a wolf in the trees but it was my imagination."

"Your imagination needs more training," his dad said crossly. "You better guard the sheep for an extra hour tonight."

Peter was annoyed.

Two nights later Peter decided to play the same trick. His father was in the house when he heard "Wolf! Wolf! Wolf! Help!" Grabbing his shotgun he raced to the field and was joined by his friends and neighbours. They were very angry when there was no wolf to be found.

Peter's dad was furious. "You must learn not to cause trouble like that!" he scolded. "You can stay on guard for the rest of the night – perhaps that will teach you a lesson."

"But, Dad, it's dark and cold," Peter moaned.

"I know," his dad replied, "but you must learn to mind the sheep properly."

As the night passed Peter felt cold and lonely. Then he heard it. A wolf howl! He peered through the darkness and was horrified to see a pack of wolves streaming towards the sheep. "Wolf!" he cried. "Wolf, wolf! Help, wolf!"

Back at the house Peter's father was woken by the shouts. "Peter has not learned his lesson yet," he said to Peter's mother. "Leave him for now," she replied. "We will talk to him about it in the morning." The neighbours also heard Peter's shouts but they all thought the same and snuggled beneath the bedclothes, ignoring Peter's cries. When he realised there was no help coming, Peter took to his heels and hid in the barn, closing the door behind him. He cried himself to sleep.

The following morning, Peter's father and neighbours were horrified to see their sheep had been attacked. "I'm very sorry, Dad," Peter said. "I know it was my own fault that no one came to help."

Peter never told anybody a lie or played silly tricks on people again.

QUIZ – FIFTH TWENTY

1 What word describes what boxers exchange and what the wind does?
2 Where is Davy Jones' Locker?
3 Who killed Goliath?
4 What does ESB stand for?
5 What is a penny farthing?
6 What name is given to the group of three islands off the coast of Clare and Galway?
7 The mermaid is said to be half-woman and half-what?
8 What is an Innuit's dome-shaped ice house called?
9 What is the German engineer Rudolf Diesel famous for inventing?
10 What was Moby Dick?
11 The cub scout leader has a special name taken from the Rudyard Kipling book, *Jungle Book*. What is it?
12 What is a small feathered fish hook usually called?
13 What is the name of Superman's girlfriend?
14 Who was the leader of the Nazi party in Germany?
15 Which cartoon character is famous for saying, "What's up, Doc"?
16 Name four of the seven dwarfs.
17 What do astronomers study?
18 What do you call an instrument for measuring air pressure?
19 Who were changed into swans by their stepmother?
20 What do you call the small triangular, coloured flags hung in rows along streets at times of celebration and festivity?

CUB HIKE GAME

With this game you can enjoy all the fun and excitement of a camping trip while sitting at home by your fireside. All you need is a dice and a different colour button for each player.

The following pages contain the game and a set of paper game cards containing instructions. Make an enlarged photocopy of both the game and the card pages. Glue the game to a piece of card and neatly trim off the edges. Glue the enlarged copy of the game cards to a piece of lighter-weight card and cut along the dotted lines. This way, you will not have to damage your book and you can take your game with you on camp or to your friends – and you will always have an original in case you lose your made-up game.

The cards are shuffled and placed in a pile on the game card square on the board.

To begin, each player throws the dice. The player throwing the highest number goes first. Play moves clockwise from this person. Moves are made forward one square for each point shown on the dice. A player throwing a six does **not** get another throw.

When a player's button lands on a shaded square he or she picks a card. Most of the cards are easily understood, bringing you forward or back some squares as notified. When a player throws a high enough number to pass an opponent they may do so, unless they are on the restricted areas on the top and bottom of the game. Here they can only go as far as the square behind their opponent.

If a player picks one of the "PASS" cards they hold it until it is needed.

When this player comes to the restriction they pass their opponent as if on the wide section. The card is then placed on the used pile. If the dice throw causes the player to land on an opponent they go forward one more square, blocking the way on him. When a player lands on another counter on the wide part of the board both players remain on the square together.

A player picking a short cut card holds it until he or she reaches the short cut. After entering the short cut the card must be returned to the used card pile and and the player continues on the squares of the short cut using dice throws.

If all cards are used before the game ends, shuffle and use them again. The game is won by the player who reaches the GONE HOME sign first. An exact throw is not needed to finish the game – if a player is three squares from the end he or she may throw a five to win the game.

Good luck, and enjoy your hike through the woods with your friends!

Help young homesick cub by chatting to her. Go forward 5.	Overtake one opponent in restriction.	Spot tracking sign which was partly hidden. Go forward 3.	Help to collect wood for campfire. Go forward 3.	Share lunch with cub who forgot his. Go forward 5.	Careful use of map and compass helped you find shortcut. Use it when you reach it.	Find wallet and give it to Akela. Go forward 5.
Careful use of map and compass helped you find shortcut. Use it when you reach it.	Entertain pack with campfire story. Go forward 4.	Help carry cub with sore ankle. Go forward 4.	Use first aid to clean and cover graze of cub who fell. Go forward 5.	Overtake one opponent in restriction.	Catch and help cook fish for supper. Go forward 4.	Stop cub friend pulling bark from tree by explaining this will kill tree. Go forward 5.
You forgot to pack your mug and plate. Miss a turn while waiting for another cub to finish.	A stone you threw bounced off a tree and hit you. Back to start for first-aid.	Tear map while squabbling with other cubs. Go back 5.	A stone you threw bounced off a tree and hit you. Back to start for first aid.	Mis-read compass. Go back 4.	Ask if any help is needed while supper is being prepared. Go forward 4.	Carry haversack for smaller cub who is tired. Go forward 5.
You have been eating sweets which you hid from the pack. Get sick. Go back 5.	Burnt fingers while messing with campfire. Go back 7.	You wandered away from the pack and caused a delay. Go back 5.	Fell in river due to not heeding Akela's warning. Back to start for change of clothes.	Rain! You left your coat in youth hostel. Go back 3.	You tied your haversack top with a granny knot. Very difficult to open. Go back 2.	Did not listen carefully to Akela – instructions unknown. Go back 5.
			You opened a gate and left it open. Cattle escape. Go back 6.	Dropped litter. Spend one hour clearing all litter in sight. Go back 5.	You packed too much in your haversack. It is too heavy. Go back 2.	You went to bed late the night before the hike. Tired and cranky. Go back 3.

QUIZ ANSWERS

First Twenty

1 ⊙
2 Pure
3 West
4 The ozone layer
5 Sherlock Holmes
6 The cuckoo
7 A burn is from dry heat, a scald is from hot liquid or steam.
8 The Shannon
9 Refer to An Óige handbook
10 Two masks – one sad, one happy
11 Mount Everest
12 Check knot
13 February
14 Local knowledge
15 A lemon
16 Flags
17 There are five: Ash, Elm, Fir, Oak, Yew
18 Robert Baden Powell
19 Rudyard Kipling
20 A type of bat

Second Twenty

1 Six
2 Three hundred and sixty

five days (1 year)
3 The Statue of Liberty
4 A sundial
5 Paris
6 Alexander Graham Bell
7 Roald Dahl
8 North-East
9 Ludwig Van Beethoven
10 V.D.U.
11 999
12 Michelle Smith
13 Japan
14 The deer
15 64
16 It is a constellation of stars visible in the night sky south of the equator
17 The New Zealand rugby team – they wear an all-black strip
18 Unidentified Flying Object
19 Kildare
20 Neither. It's an Indian dish of curried fish!

Third Twenty

1 Phoenix Park – Dublin
2 The Ha'penny Bridge
3 The Rolls Royce
4 Westmeath

5 Six miles
6 Gold, Silver and Bronze
7 March 17th
8 Local knowledge
9 • • • — — — • • •
10 Yellow
11 A bull
12 South
13 The shutter
14 Amhrán Na bhFiann (The Soldier's Song)
15 Jamboree
16 Paris
17 1014
18 Italy
19 The oak
20 The salmon

Fourth Twenty
1 Oisín
2 The Lee
3 The News
4 Anna Sewell
5 Sugar
6 On a mountain
7 Blue
8 Cry
9 A spider
10 The harp
11 Eight
12 This answer changes every few years
13 Libra
14 Round

15 Stamps
16 Six
17 Kerry
18 Kilkenny
19 Holland
20 No, it's a mammal

Fifth Twenty
1 Blows
2 It's the sailor's name for the bottom of the sea
3 David
4 Electricity Supply Board
5 A bicycle
6 The Aran Islands
7 Fish
8 An igloo
9 The diesel engine
10 A white whale in the book *Moby Dick* by Herman Melville
11 Akela — pronounced A-kay-la
12 A fly
13 Lois Lane
14 Adolf Hitler
15 Bugs Bunny
16 Sleepy, Grumpy, Bashful, Doc, Happy, Dopey, Sneezy
17 Outer Space
18 A barometer
19 The Children of Lir
20 Bunting

PUZZLE PAGES
····················

Cub Wordsearch page 32

K	T	E	O	C	S	I	X	E	R
I	O	U	K	N	Q	I	R	E	O
L	N	T	O	N	K	Q	X	O	P
T	L	A	R	G	H	I	L	L	E
O	A	E	P	L	S	T	S	A	E
U	R	M	K	C	M	B	A	L	B
C	A	M	D	O	A	P	U	U	U
L	O	S	N	I	T	M	A	C	K

Crossword Solution page 33
Across
1 Pack 3 Riser 7 Creep
8 Engine 10 A.T.M . 12 Toe
17 School 20 India 21 Ennis
22 Camp

Down
1 Pine 2 Crag 3 Race
4 Scent 5 Rope 6 One
9 Nut 11 Mao 13 Olden
14 B.C.G. 15 Fire 16 Taps
18 Orca 19 Loop

Mystery Word page 34
Tie, Eel, Nap, Top, Pie, Owl,
Lip, Eat, Sun.
The first letters of these words

spell out the word
TENTPOLES

Names Mix-Up page 34
Antrim, Galway, Shannon,
Leinster, Kerry, Tyrone,
Rosslare, Liffey, Donegal, Louth,
Wexford, Kildare.
Coded Message page 35
"A good cub always does their
best"

Gold Island page 49
The Gold Island treasure is at
the western edge of Galeforce
Forest.